# *Blue Collar*
# EULOGIES

# *Blue Collar* EULOGIES

## MICHAEL MEYERHOFER

STEEL TOE BOOKS BOWLING GREEN, KENTUCKY

ISBN 978-0-9824169-0-7

STEEL TOE BOOKS
Western Kentucky University
Department of English
1906 College Heights Blvd. #11086
Bowling Green, KY 42101-1086
steeltoebooks.com

COVER PHOTO
"Subway" by Kara Thurmond, 2008
karathurmond.com

COVER AND BOOK DESIGN
Molly McCaffrey

This book is dedicated to all those whose friendship and influence helped make this possible, including: Allison Joseph, Dorianne Laux, George Bilgere, Rodney Jones, Judy Jordan, Joan Dy, Amy Blache, Tom Hunley, Lesley Doyle, and my family (both past and present), along with quite a few strangers, ghosts, critics, bartenders, dead writers, non-emo musicians, inanimate objects, and The History Channel.

Wanting to go to the eastern cliff
setting out now after how many years
yesterday I used the vines to pull myself up
but halfway there wind and mist made the going tough
the narrow path grabbed at my shoes
the moss so slippery I couldn't proceed
so I stopped right here beneath this cinnamon tree
used a cloud as a pillow and went to sleep

—HAN SHAN, DATE UNKNOWN

# Contents

### III. DIAGNOSING GOD

# IV. REAL COURAGE

# I. THE TROUBLE WITH HAMMERS

# THE TROUBLE WITH HAMMERS

The trouble with owning hammers
is that you have to store them somewhere,
on pegs or at least in a drawer
or inside an emptied out tackle box,
long after the house is built
and the circus folded like an envelope
on the backs of unfamiliar trucks, running
all night from Maine to Hollywood.
I want to go by three names
like child actors and serial killers.
My father kept hammers in a drawer
and once, when he stopped by
but I was out, he nailed a two-by-four
he stole from a construction site
under the sagging cushions of my couch.
I keep my hammers in the closet
but he found them anyway. I would
like to be a hammer, I think,
and swing all day down on the heads
of thin, unsuspecting nails
even though I am not particularly
violent or unmedicated, if that matters.
It's true, I was never any good
at math, ever since that one bronze
star in fifth grade, and I know
you're not supposed to begin a speech
or say in a poem how nervous
you are, but I think there are more nails
than people, and more hammers

3

than people, and I am weary of these
constant reminders that nothing
built after the pyramids
seems able to hold together for long—
not just relationships, but other things
like bookshelves, governments,
the new consensus on circumcision.
They say Man's first tool was a hammer,
which makes sense since I can't
imagine apes working a protractor,
much like a sextant under the wet stars.
But each time I swing, I can feel
my own head loosen from its shaft
of lacquered bone, and I know
once it flies, it will never be tight again.

# THE CLAY-SHAPER'S HUSBAND

Here I am, confronting this bowl
kept under guard and pressurized glass
in the archway of the St. Louis Art Museum,
and somehow it feels good
to note that it's not all that impressive.

Clean, sure, and smooth, but plain.
Like this is just the demonstration piece
by the teacher of a pottery class
who has fired his kiln so many times
he could—and does—do it while drunk.

Then I see the note on the plaque
that says this was made by a woman,
which apparently they can tell
by the curves petrified within the swirl-print.
That, I decide, must explain the absence

of a hunt-carving. Say, a bison
turned sideways in an empty field
while some scrawny fool hefts a spear
that looks, coincidentally, about as thick
as his own and the bison's legs.

But this one lacks adornment,                                      5
which is a nice way of saying it's boring
to someone raised on video games,
who nods off in movie theaters
whenever spaceships stop exploding.

Now should be the story's turn
where I visualize the ancient woman
who shaped this and try
to pull off some simple, heroic ending
that shows her bronze wrists

deep in Nile-mud, hair up, her infant crying
because that's what infants do
—especially in 2000 B.C.
without canned applesauce and Pedialyte.
I am leaving the museum now.

Giving up, I think not of my clay-shaper
but the men next to her. How one, at least,
must have thought it a miracle
when her small hands rounded the earth
and left it that way. How could he know better?

Perhaps this was the same man
whose eyes drew lines between the stars
while the others laughed at him.
No one saw the hunter, the bull, the ladle
no matter how he pointed.

But *she* saw, I bet. That's why
she gave him that bulb of pottery
the size of a baby cabbage.
*Here*, she said. *Love what you can touch.*
And he did, washing her small hands like jewels.

6

# THE CRAYON NOT TAKEN

I am the child in third grade
who, right before Thanksgiving, accidentally
colored his drawing of a pumpkin green,
and I've come back to tell you
that, too, can make all the difference.

You are the girl who snickered,
safe behind what you dutifully made orange
with just some green fringe on top,
who teased me before you grabbed your coat
and rushed off to your waiting parents.

On the way to your grandmother's,
you told them about the stupid boy in class
who forgot what color pumpkins were,
and because you always played by the rules,
now you are wealthy and married.

I, on the other hand, have lived
in the backseat of a '99 Cavalier in late July,
when heat melts the life from seeds
and, because it has no place else to go,
it wrestles through the soil for air.

True, we both went to college,
suffered loves and crises like fevers;
the difference being that only one of us knows
how awful it is in third grade
to forget what color pumpkins are.

Who sees them when he closes his eyes
—green, always green. In patches
grown as large as your head, but back then,
in the columns of third grade art class,
no bigger than the size of your heart.

## SAMSARA

I still dream about
Stan's Drive-In on East Main,
that grease-dive where,
for three teenage summers,
I flipped burgers
and broasted chicken
soaked in ice-cold marinade,
washing dishes
and scooping fistfuls
of pickles into jars
while the owner flirted
with girls in loose tank-tops
who leaned over counters
and car windows
and made twice what I did.

Always the same—
back from teaching, books
and a Master's degree
under my belt, but suddenly
I'm broke, so back I go
to knotting aprons
and buttering dinner rolls,
trying my best
to ignore the temper
of the owner, who popped
like hot oil whenever
too many orders
poured in and reminded him
of his drill sergeant.

Nothing has changed:
freezer burn, bent tongs,
putrid back-musk of the drain
whenever someone
flushes the kitchen toilet.
But once in awhile,
it rains and traffic lulls
and some bored, pretty girl
who doesn't know me
gets tired of handling sundaes,
says she wants to learn
how to fry a corndog.
Back she comes, and for once,
I have all the answers.

# HOLLYWOOD JACK

I am tired of men named Jack
locking swords with pirates, falling in love
on the decks of sea-faring death-traps,
traveling to parallel worlds
to challenge exiled Egyptian gods.

Always the same story—Jack
must come out of retirement to perform
spinal surgery on a crying child,
then lead a manhunt after stolen nukes
before acknowledging his feelings

for a fellow rancher whose hat
perfectly matches the color of his horse.
You've seen Jack many times
since he axed that giant beanstalk—
he has the best one-liners,

earns hegemony over desert islands,
wrestles angels by the throat
then saves brunettes from runaway trains.
He is the one who gets too involved.
He is the skeleton who loves Christmas.

He is the coiled jester inside boxes.
Sometimes, he inspires strangers to dance,
steal, lift things, masturbate.
That show-hoarding verb of a man
who goes through sidekicks like syllables.

See what he's done to pumpkins,
forests, how he's infiltrated every deck
of playing cards—bowing still
to the hoity king and queen, sometimes
the ace, but it's only a matter of time.

## ONE HIT WONDERS

Still ages before the invention
of the blistering guitar solo,

back when rock music consisted,
literally, of rocks

clattering down a hillside
or shaping the palm of some river

not yet given a name—
probably the hero back then

was whoever threw the first spear
through an elk's snowy hide,

or cupped water inside
a dead thing's busted skull.

See how his face reflects
when he carries his creation

back to the others, how they lift him
on the shoulders of their praise,

how they won't let him go
until he outdoes his own miracle.

## BPM 37093

Separated by fifty-odd light years
from the Star of Africa
lies a celestial jewel 2,500 miles across,
carats on the order of ten billion
followed by twenty-four more zeros.
A smoldering white dwarf
like our own pyrite-colored sun may be.
Proof that after a solar relationship
ends, like most relationships,
with a fiery, bloating rampage
followed by a crash-diet
down to blistered, white-hot corestuff,
the leftover carbon crystallizes
into a two-septillion-ton rock
set in an orbital band of dark ether.
Scientists learned this, they say,
because diamond-stars ring like gongs,
yielding signals that pulse
like the quintessential last word
of bodies long since scalded to cinders.

## LIMBIC SELF-LOATHING,
## POST EMPEROR'S CHICKEN

I almost forgot about the stone penguin
left under my bed after the tornado,
which you gave me after my father and I
sought shelter in your storm cellar,
rappelling down a cable into the darkness.
And since this was the dream-world,
it made sense that I'd see you again, Lisa,
whom I haven't thought about in years
and was never, I think, in love with
although in my dream, I was disarmed
by your charitable grin, waving
in your Future Farmers of America tee,
during what it took for my neural firestorm
to shock me back up to consciousness.
We were driving along Iowa back-roads
when the tornado touched down
on the barren gravel, spared us by looking,
then I saw you in the distance
and pled shelter into your storm cellar.
So you gave me a stone penguin
to remember you by, which I then kept
under my bed for reasons that made sense
at the time. I'll also say, since readers
of poetry are either lovers or haters
of Freud, that the penguin's bill
was erect as a cavalryman's saber,
that I had trouble rappelling down your cellar
which was, in turns out, a swamped pit,

that your ex-marine father did not approve
but your mother found me charming,
and that you—that girl I'd forgotten
until I dreamt about her—chose another.

## ANNIVERSARY

*"Who was the second man to walk on the moon?"*

—*trivia question*

The headlines say that Mars
will swing within forty-four million miles
tonight, its first time that close
since two years ago, which happened to be
the closest in six thousand decades.

It's hard not to be disappointed
when big events puppy-dog greater ones.
Take Elisha Gray, for instance,
who invented the telephone but applied
just hours late for a patent. Or

that Hebrew prophet of the same name,
multiplying a widow's jars of oil
after Elijah rode a chariot into heaven,
forgotten now like whatever
Edison invented after the lightbulb,
like the Thespians killed at Thermopylae.

Let's remember the Maginot Line, for once.
What the Nazis learned from Armenia.
What I have not learned from love.
Outside, a fingernail of orange
sails down night's shale-dust runway.

17

The crater-tongues of Syrtis Major.
Mons Olympus, that lord of volcanoes.
Phobos and Deimos, tiny moons
skimming the ether like sand dollars.
And us, almost as beautiful as last year.

## ODE TO DOGS

I am tired of hearing about dogs
used as metaphors for the uncivilized.
Imagine a world in which humans

possessed at least twenty times
as many olfactory receptors,
able to distinguish the tang of cancer

rising musk-like from the bedsheets
next to a smoldering ash tray,
able to detect that one drop of blood

in every five quarts of water,
to know what you did last night
no matter how many times

you soap-scrubbed the evidence.
It does not take savagery
but more love than we can muster

to lick the hand you've sniffed,
to love despite the perfume of sins
we wear each day like a halo.

# AGAINST ETYMOLOGY

At *dark, I make a homesick*
says the Japanese exchange student
in my lover's ESL class,
writing how much he misses
his family, his girlfriend,
a certain café in Kyoto.
I suggest tutoring. But that night,
it feels strangely fitting
after our second bottle of wine
to cap the red pen
bleeding cursive
from her palms and lead her
into the bedroom. *Let's make sleep,*
I whisper—and we lie
still sheathed in our clothes,
two bodies fused like Latin roots
while a full moon
the color of vegetable stock
unfurls its approval,
shimmering through curtains
that shadow us—yes—
like clapping paper fans.

## HAUNTED

Again, I find myself
back in the halls of high school,
trying to remember which
red tin locker is mine
and worse yet, the combination
to get the book
for the test I'm late for
in a class I forgot I even had,
and by the way,
where the hell my pants are.
They say I should accept
that I will always be tree-ringed
by the first bully's shove,
that first Gestapo-like snicker
of the cornflower girl
who unintentionally taught me
the sorry mechanics of love.
So too they tell me that
dying will be like going to sleep,
that old cosmic sales pitch
about death being
not a period, but a comma.
When I die, I think it will be
like falling sideways into water.
Which we can breathe,
all of us—until we try.

# II. THE FIRST KILL

## THE FIRST KILL

When Grandfather shot his first buck
of the season, a great leg-tangled
nine-point raised on wheat-fetch and fields
of rain-slogged cornwaste, he sawed off
its sorry head and nailed it as-is
above the garage door, so that for months
afterward, Sunday visits meant braving
flesh-flies, down-shed tatters of hide
and sinew frozen stiff in winter's papyrus,
droppings stewed in snowmelt until
sagegrass sprung from driveway gravel,
and that breeze-blasted deer skull
loomed clean as a footprint overhead.

I was nine. In church, flushed priests
said Christ turned Jew-water into wine
and hailed rotten Lazarus from the grave,
even as sag-breasted schoolmarms
chalked out the cell walls of plants and
taught us how the universe was stretching
like a lie from its bedrock of nothing,
hinged like the bones of dinosaurs
and the skulls of schoolboys on matter,
sunlight, this many calories and hormones
kicking growth from a mother-seed
that once roamed wild through still fields,
awaiting the doom of its own birth.

## BLUE COLLAR EULOGY

Neck-deep in a lecture on anaphora,
tired of the tie I still can't pull off,
suddenly I hear myself telling my students

how we used to be homeless:
my mother, a failed librarian tethered
to the chirp of a dialysis machine

like angels to the will of God. My father,
a weightlifter who found Christ
hiding inside the state penitentiary.

My brother's father, a surgeon
who let himself out of her dorm room
at Loras College just as easily

as he wandered from her life. How,
for a time, dirt-broke in the backwaters,
my father busted loading pallets

all day for salvage cost, sweat
combing the fin-hairs along his triceps.
Then, at night, scouted the county

for abandoned houses, tin-roof shacks
where we lived sometimes weeks
before they found us. How we weathered

whole years on government cheese
and russet tapwater. But I don't tell them
the worst of it—how a bent spine

kept me in diapers, how I hated
whatever jerk of blue collar jism made me
this way. Half-eared, limping,

in my heart a carnival freak
hefting a protest sign outside Nirvana.
A Roman of conscience, sort of,

carving my palm with a switchblade
because pills cost more than bread.
No, it's enough they note how

mosquitoes tremble in the sun-silt.
How flowers with Latin names
grow best from graves, from junkyards

where they rise slowly and forget
the sin they made in hating the earth.
The earth, that feeds as best it can.

## MY FRIEND AND I PLAY
## THE WHITE MAN'S BLUES

My friend, older than I am,
says life in the seventies was good
so long as you were white
and male; otherwise, not so much,
but allegedly it's gotten better.
Meaning worse for us—
and yes, it's about damn time.
Still, how not to long for the day
when shy, one-eared, weightlifting
poets like me could find
decent jobs just by walking
through some manager's door?
True, I've never had much,
not even an address sometimes,
and all my efforts to teach
poetry result in letters
that begin with *Dear Applicant.*
But it was only a year ago
that our president took some time
to groom his Clydesdales
and play golf while black families
in New Orleans drowned
in their attics. My friend shoots
his discolored whiskey, lowers the glass,
says we should riot or something.
I say he's right. Let's do it.
But then, the jukebox changes songs.
The waitress makes her rounds.
Outside it rains, stops, rains again.

# HUNGER, 1995

It was the summer between tragedies
and I wanted a part-time job,
so I crossed the maple-webbed sidewalk
outside this stalled shopping mall
and filled out a Temporary Services app.

I used the office phone to call home
because I didn't know my social security
number, then took a test involving
shaded cubes turned inside out
like the belly of a hypothetical shark.

Finally, a typing test. I was a virgin,
anchored between crushes on cheerleaders
and equally unattainable Playmates,
so I'd written enough bad poems
to leave the keyboard smoking.

They smiled, said I was qualified
to do data entry for seven bucks an hour—
twice what I made baling hay
in the throat-jagging fog of barn lofts.
I waited while they wrote down directions.

Then this old woman walked in,
pushing the tin bell's sound before her.
She said she'd just retired
from marriage because her husband died
and her savings was a Dust Bowl.

A computer? She'd never seen one.
But she could mop or change a diaper
if they'd find her something
within a bus stop or two of home.
I cannot tell you what happened next

because I left, walked home,
daydreaming for once of good things.
Women, paychecks, a getaway car.
Meanwhile, the mosquitoes followed,
looking for something bare to eat.

# TIMELINE

If *now* means me sitting here
with frayed chopsticks and warm sushi,
trying to feign a scholar's glow,

then Friday was my Renaissance
because this blonde's merciful neckline
left me flustered as those

Frenchmen who studied Greek
then rushed off, mad, to paint something.
Thus, Tuesday was my Dark Age

because it went almost exactly
the way Monday did, raw earth rolling
like a Celt's shield until Sunday

faded the color of stone. I guess
you could call last year my Mesozoic
because my heart had knuckles

but no words, no way to pine
for days when childhood, like Pangaea,
seemed more or less fine

on retrospect. *It's the Precambrian*
*that haunts you most*, says my therapist.
And I imagine I can feel

that ancient, one-celled bacteria
Democritus mistook for a soul
crawling from its shell—already a fossil

recycled from when I swam
in dark matter and drank so hard
I dragged myself inside out into light.

## SELF-AMPUTATION

Today, my family calls
to tell me my grandfather just tried
ending it all with a shotgun.

*Well, this is the day,* he announced,
but grabbed the wrong gauge
from the closet shot-box.

Back when I was fifteen, he said
his legs hurt him so much
he was about to saw them off,

showed me ankles soaking
like blue stems in his penny-loafers.
What do you say to that?

But my legs didn't work either,
at least not enough to play football
meaning not enough to get laid

in Baptist towns where Christ
hangs alongside the Southern Cross.
By the time I left home,

I'd learned how to ignore him,
could even diagnose his disorders
because I had them too.

Once, I gave a suicide poem
to my parents. They walked away.
Like you, I know the turn

of a locked door, the weight
of a sealed box, that you never
grab the wrong gauge by accident.

## UNREQUITED

By high school, I'd developed
what I thought was a handsome stare.
Meaning I tucked my chin,
furrowed my thick German eyebrows
like an aspiring Tom Cruise
and gazed hard at the one I liked.
Problem was, I always held
a second or three too long
and took on the countenance of a stalker
or, in the case of class pictures,
a homicidal Amish boy with bad hair.
I had no fashion sense, either.
Then again, this was northern Iowa
where women wear daisies to funerals
and grace belongs to roosters
who catwalk their plumage
between burgundy schoolhouses
and silos packed tight with cornrot.
I've learned a little since then
about myself, less about the figments
with Swedish breasts and Wrangler jeans
who crowded every calendar but mine.
I am not asking for your pity
although I'll take what I can get—
this being one of many lessons
whispered by firelight at keg parties
in the perfume of a plowed field,
back when legs and Mellencamp spread
like gossip as I shucked about,
bleary-eyed, frowning at everything.

## LANDMARKS

I bought a bag of all black socks
with my twenty-first birthday money,
thinking this would save me
from having to match them, sure,
but also the embarrassment
of wearing white ones to a funeral
like I did after my mother died—
same day my father
almost cut my left ear off
when I asked him to help me
remove the rusty latch of an earring
for years I thought was in style.
He couldn't see straight,
didn't even register my curse
when the scissors caught my lobe
until my brother stopped him.
Since I was already born
without a right ear,
for which I never blamed her
but now and again the ultrasound,
I'm grateful. My brother
tells me how he wore black jeans
to his rich girlfriend's
sister's wedding, how they laughed
so hard he had to spend
the next five years climbing
the economic ladder to Dewey Ballantine,
dinners under a ten-foot chandelier.
Today, at last, I throw out

that last pair, faded like old tires,
plus an outdated silk shirt
that reminds me of the dress
they buried my maker in. Sunflowers
permanently wrinkled by disco.
*She looks lovely,* said her old roommate,
blond with black eyebrows,
as she pulled me deep
into a midwestern bosom
perfumed by the Dollar General,
so deep I wanted to cry.
And would have, had I been
brave enough to wear the grief
my mother earned—she who daily
tamed my cowlicks with a wet comb,
even after the milk dried
and I, insufferably ignorant,
stopped believing she was God.

## THE FIRST LADY

I dreamt about Barbara Bush again. Same Betsy Ross
pantsuit, back sloped like an old seal—but this time, no
Houston Astrodome rose from the slogged skyline like
a sanitized nipple, no remarks about how proletariats
seeking shelter from a premeditated hurricane should
be used to life in cramped, shit-stained hallways. No, in
this one, she was driving her candy-red Hummer out of
Washington when she took the wrong detour, wound
up in Osage, Iowa. There she was, floating between the
tattered maples that still line Main Street, when she
missed one of only three stoplights and nearly ran over
my uncle—the one who lives in a teepee, even though
he's not Native American. To avoid scandal, she agreed
to help us shovel cow-pies. We figured she'd have one
of those burly agents with a Roman haircut take over.
But it seems the work agreed with her. White gloves,
the shovel's bright blade dyed a deeper black with each
thrust. The sun full of flies. The former First Lady
shoveling manure, humming a Monroe tune long after
the rest of us retired. When we sat down to dinner, we
could still see her through the window, transferring
filth from one field to another, dirt mending the
cracks in her face.

## THE LAST GOOD AMERICAN DECIDES NOT TO RUN FOR PRESIDENT

I wonder what those prehistoric humans used for
metaphors—so long before match-sticks, before hole-
punchers or overactive immune systems, before sun-
honeyed refugees squashed by relief crates filled with
pudding cups, when ruin meant slag-toothed tigers or
avalanching stones popping bones like bubble-wrap.
Really, I suppose it's not so different from what I pon-
dered back in high school, watching varsity wrestlers
tangle themselves in brutal, spandexed origami while
bleachers roared—who first witnessed some dispute
over a fistful of edible berries and decided headlocks
were a bright idea? Ape-haired before zoos, incontinent
before diapers, bipolar before cocaine, picture hearing
the shopping cart clatter of thunder when you couldn't
even conjure one simile, one consonant to shield your-
self. Now, with spring pimping its overblown renewal
all over our front lawns, when the ribs of trees replen-
ish their modest upholstery while biological lust flicks
on like a porch light, I begin to understand. Or rather,
not to care. Bookends, poker chips, gravity. Vague
threat of blindness from my friend's backyard wine.
The pinned stars of badges. One roll of film, acciden-
tally loaded twice—two lovers, life and death, superim-
posed. And what Americans call sense, still not worth
its own bloody homophone.

COLLATERAL DAMAGE

*From a photograph by Kael Alford*

An eight year old girl lies naked,
taut on one side, a soft arm reaching

across splotched, sandstone tiles
toward figures we cannot see

as they slowly wash her black hair.
Her navel the size of a quarter.

Her chest like a calf's underbelly.
She does not blink when clear

water bounces from her shoulders.
Could be day or night. An old woman

in a neat burka holds her steady,
squeezing her hand. A man's fistful

of lambswool unfurls from
the child's thighs. Between bones

like yours and mine, still clothed
in sleeves of olive baby-fat.

Spare me the stats on Smart Bombs,
Blackwater's mission statement,

Greenspan's stance on oil wars.
Just tell me why she does not blink.

# III.  DIAGNOSING GOD

# THE FOUNDLING

Indian summer.
Maples bloom in manicured grids,
                    box-wings unfurling
on either side
of the long, russet freight-lines

next to a squatter's shack
where a Catholic schoolboy learns
to know himself

without touch, imagining
a holy topography
the priests never taught him.

                    Night comes
with scissors, butchering
nimbus clouds still
plump with rain, waiting to be soaked

into the soiled maze of turnips
and clover—rooted deep
            where fallen angels crowd, still

mouthing
the syllable for God
with their blue, quivering lips.

## THE FIRST DANCERS

It horrified me in fifth grade to read
how ancient jellyfish evolved
into stomachs with fangs and biceps,
mosquitoes sporting javelins for stingers,
educated men knotting yellow stars
to arms still soft with baby-fat.

Whittle a few hundred million rings
from the trunk of our world's history,
then behold the iridescence
of king-sized jellyfish fanning the deep,
their feelers curling and uncurling
with a grace reserved for invertebrates.

Before the Amazon fell to loggers—
long before kindling, much less stoves—
picture schools of these peaceful dancers
roaming the depths, gelatin comets
gumming plankton. Then one grows a tooth.
It begins. It cannot be stopped.

## "SCIENTISTS DISCOVER SINGING ICEBERG IN ANTARCTICA"

*—Reuters article*

Who are we to say it isn't music
whenever an iceberg anchors down
and hums like a beehive,

an orchestra tuning itself
in the world's oldest concert hall?
Not a steady drone,

they say, but a changing melody
imperceptible to our ears
unless it's amplified, tinkered with—

much like the silence before
that first fiddle of hair on bone.
That holy day when Neanderthals

with their cattle-dark eyes
softly blew through water-reeds
to the river's wild applause.

# THE WORLD'S OLDEST FORM OF THIEVERY

*Damn Koreans keep stealing my panties*
my girlfriend says—either the shy landlord
who jogs with an iPod full of Asian rap,

or the fuchsia-haired man from Ilsan
who came by to fix her washing machine
while she was out taking pictures

of a bamboo temple in Seoul. Her black
G-string and pagan-red thong, sure,
but the plain high-cuts too—

six or seven pairs in all, plus some socks
I never knew would travel
fourteen time zones from my floor.

To clear her mind, she goes back
to climb with the pilgrims up Bukhansan—
mostly men, eyes like swans' wings,

the nearly upright path bearded
with firs in the pyrite stubble of sunrise.
The old women stir kimchi instead,

gloves stained red from gochujang
as they genuflect over burnt ceramic jugs.
Sometimes, shops attract wild dogs

to the holy foothills—they chew on the tarps
that keep the plastic verandas dry.
*This time*, she says, *the dogs were fucking*.

INTO THE DEEP

The brains of whales are bigger than ours
and more complex, they say,
and the whales dive deeper than any living thing
without machines. Deeper into the cold

dark water, miles below the light.
They float down, their bodies full of milk
and come back up, rising off the deep
like fat blue angels. But they also say

that miles farther than that,
down at the very bottom,
there are creatures
who have never seen the light.

There are creatures
no bigger than your daughter's thumbnail
who do not breathe air.
Who have never heard of the Kingston Trio

or the *Voyager* space probes.
Nomads of an abyss
so deep that stars do not exist.
They float in colonies or live alone,

mouths with feet,
without knowledge of what wheels
through the heavens above
or me, and how tonight

for reasons known only
to this poem, I draw a steaming bath
and sink in, mile by mile,
until something within me breaks

and then unfolds—stretching
its ancient webbing between this world
and the last, between gods
and the science they left behind.

DIAGNOSING GOD

*"Let there be Light!"* –Genesis, 1:3

I wonder what phobia made God
so surly in that ancient world,

prescribing locusts and brimstone
one day, circumcision the next.

Perhaps a case of teratophobia,
fear of making deformed children,

which my mother did not share
although I fell shy of God's image,

born limp-finned as a boned fish,
and that transgression cost her life.

Or pogonophobia, fear of beards,
manifest when the universe cooled

into billion-mile hairs of starlight.
Scopophobia—why no one may see

the face of God and live, although
too many still pray for such ruin.

Remember that sand-plowed bluff
when Moses asked his name—

I wonder if sesquipedalophobia,
fear of long words, applies as well.

Overcompensation for patroiphobia
could explain those geneologies

but imagine, if you can, the torment
of a divine uranophobe, detesting

the very heavens he presides over.
I could love a god with ecclesiophobia,

for I too have been afraid of churches;
still, as death—that cardiophobe—

unfurls his plans for my demise,
I have better things to do than

sympathize for the one scotophobe
who could flare his darting eyes

in all that insufferable darkness
and purge it with just four words.

## JESUS RETURNS TO THE WORLD
## WITH AMNESIA AND TRIES TO
## LIVE A NORMAL LIFE

I gave up bread and strong wine,
but still I feel a strange sickness
whenever the sun gilds a new
interstate or a pasture of dark-eyed
cattle silently flipping their tails,
the poor dears, like fallen gods.

At the gym, a pretty college girl
on the elliptical looked like
she had not eaten in forty days,
ribs straining underneath
a rainbow leotard, bronze skin
stretched over bags of silicone.

I could not bear her painted eyes,
the feeling when she smiled at me
or afterwards, when I got home,
how my computer had been hijacked
by pop-ups for diet pills, offers
to add more girth to my manhood.

Later, I wonder was it ever easier
as my wife wheels out our new
baby boy from the hospital with a cloudy
bandage in place of his foreskin,
joking that now, she'll have less
to cringe over when changing him.

Dear Lord, it's getting hard to care
that dreams burn up like paper cranes,
that my wrists ache when it hails
and I wonder what kind of terrible age
we've all been cast into—but no,
I think, it has always been like this.

## SCATOMANCY

I have been thinking for days now
that I must tell you more
about that night, driving home
from New Orleans, when I stopped
by a Wal-Mart at midnight
to use the men's room and found
the walls—all one of them—
smeared thick with feces.
Of course, I can only assume
it was human, since I did not have
a chemistry kit, nor the stomach
to risk someone walking in
and blaming me, the way late arrivals
always blame the murder
on the first guy who finds the body.
I know how imprudent it is
to pin my dharma to stuff
we flush faster than wedding vows,
but my friends who heard this
told me once, they found their daughter
grinning from the open hatch
of her crib, having just finger-painted
herself and the nearest walls
with acrid fistfuls of her own self-serve.
Without going any further
than a tub framed in paper lilacs,
they bathed her clean again.
I hear now, she's reading the dictionary,
having long since forgotten

how once, she was terribly proud
of her discovery—not of words,
not even sound, but matter.
The most primal of God's tongues,
delivered from the inside out.

# SNOWMAN

Not a snowman—a snow *sculpture*.
That's how friends described it afterwards.
The Buddha in repose, smiling,
hands folded between his bare knees.

It was two years before Armageddon,
according to televangelists. I was trying
as the millennium wound down
to reevaluate my beliefs and get laid.

The anonymous sculptor gave the Buddha
a snow-dais, holding him aloft
in the middle of that blank frisbee field
across from Mayflower, our dorm.

I thought I was in love that weekend.
Southern Iowa, dead of February
where some of the drifts reached my belt.
The river stopped, a petrified ribbon.

The redhead I wrote poems for
had a three-way with my roommates
while I tried to distract myself
by reading Bashó over Jack Daniels.

Even his fingernails were perfect.
Bulge of the femur where his knees bent.
Closed eyelids, smooth as silk,
concealing the pupil of some mystery

it would be years before I understood.
All my poems failed in iambs.
The redhead I was in love with,
whose breasts jostled when she walked,

said once she wanted to read them.
When no one would answer
the door, I slumped outside, erased
that knowing smile with my gloved fist.

## ELEGY FOR A HORSE'S ASS

Once, when my father was driving
through thick, rural darkness
down a ribbon of highway south of St. Paul,
a retired Clydesdale strayed
from its pasture of hay and clover,
right into the blind spot
of a teenage girl air-drying her Porsche.
My father saw the whole thing—
how the windshield broke like applause,
how a helicopter lifted her to Mayo
in a lattice of white straps.
How men had to chainsaw the horse
just to reach her. Afterwards,
the pieces shoved off
like the soggy halves of a tuna melt.
A cop with a flashlight beckoning traffic.
The horse's hind quarters
rumping the ditch-weed, like it started
to burrow underground
then got stuck. Couldn't back up.
*Hell of a sight,* my father says.
I don't tell him I feel this way too
when I write, like a humanized ostrich
or, if you prefer, a horse's ass
tunneling between worlds
while strangers gawk,
streaming past, honking in tongues.

# ODE TO A TROJAN

I still wonder sometimes
what couple left their used condom
in the playground woodchips

of Sacred Heart Catholic School—
just left it there to be found by a gang
of fourth-graders at recess,

autumn weighing the fluted limbs
of summer-sapped maples,
an unkempt sleeve encircled

by boys and girls who barely knew
the depth of the world's sin,
believing still in corporeal dogma.

Our teacher pinned it to a twig
snapped from a thirty-something limb,
carried it off like a soiled Pamper.

We stared, enthralled, our bodies
still soft as fresh-born lambs.
God knows what made them come

to our consecrated playground
the night before, moon spilling through
the aluminum hieroglyphs

of swing-sets and tornado-slides.
I wonder if rebellion drove their lust,
or if it was just appreciation

for moon-lit fields shielded
from traffic by wrinkled woodwinds,
for the silky clumsiness of night

air and in the distance, the church
whose stain-glass windows
look almost peaceful in the dark.

# IV. REAL COURAGE

## REAL COURAGE

I think I could be very brave
under the right circumstances. For instance
if I were in the middle of lifting weights
shirtless in front of a mirror
and the Wolfman broke in, conveniently
just as I was pausing to admire
my silver-plated crossbow set; or else
if I happened to stroll onto the roof
of a clock-tower about the time a glass-jawed sniper
was fumbling with a jammed rifle,
or a shipload of hostile aliens
or a van filled with terrorists and nail-bombs
stalled in the middle of an oil field
while I palmed my cigarette lighter, then,
*then* I could be every bit as brave
as the indestructible Achilles. I would pose
for sculptors, glossy movie posters, a fan club
full of pipe-smoking intellectuals, silky-
tongued critics and well-breasted gymnasts
hanging on my every word and deed.

But in the real world, vampires only attack
while you're sitting on the toilet
or trying on your mother's high heels;
muggers only leap from the rosebushes
when you're ducking out of a cheap motel
or leaving Family Video with armloads
of porn. And if the State wants you dead,
if they send a death-squad of cyborgs

or a serial killer marks you in the parking lot,
it will happen when you're constipated.
You'll not have bathed or shaved yet,
paramedics will note your frayed underpants,
an absent testicle, the acne your face wore
as you piled into a car full of burger wrappers
and the day-old remnants of diet shakes,
unconcerned with collapsing elevators
or damsels on runaway horses, derailed trains
and earthbound asteroids, unprepared
to meet your maker but willing to finish
without fanfare, getting by as best you can.

## FOR MY NINTH BIRTHDAY

They gave me a paper castle
when my mother went in for surgery—
a children's book of turrets
I was supposed to cut out, fold, glue
then populate with knuckle-sized
peasants in dresses and jerkins.
From this, I was to learn
the grace of imagined worlds,
that books have four dimensions.

With patience I've since lost,
I raised the lion banners and parapets,
the red-haired maiden's bower,
fixed the menacing portcullis
in front of what I did not yet know
were called murder holes
for the archers kneeling above,
listening to fake minstrels play while
my family paced by the phone.

I gave each of the knights names,
doted over their bright tabards
and eternally drawn blades,
put down green construction paper
so their horses could graze,
imagined enemies massing somewhere
beyond the edge of the coffee table
like a storm they could not see,
like a tragedy only I could prevent.

## THE GROUNDSKEEPERS

Because no one else would do it,
the town hired a pack of high school
boys to tend the hilltop cemetery
three hours every summer morning,
unsupervised for a poverty wage.

Instead, they tackled headstones,
trying to heave them onto the grass,
leaving thin cracks in the angels' skirts
that families blamed on humidity
or poor workmanship. Meanwhile

the boys rode lawnmowers through
bouquets of white roses, forget-me-nots,
returned after dark to climb the wire
fence with its sturdy padlock and build
bonfires at the heart of the cemetery.

Sometimes they brought girls along,
cleavage straining from Goodwill halters
while meager paychecks transformed
into lukewarm Pabst and Busch, passed
between bare hands like communion.

Later, the boys fought by moonlight
until the girls soothed them with whispers,
gliding off behind the gloomy trees
and shadows bristling with headstones.
The next morning, the boys

always met by the equipment shed,
youth charming them from hangovers,
curses still streaming from their lips—
somehow overnight, the grass
on the graves had grown long again.

## GRIEF SONG

I poured my mother's ashes like gravy
on a nest of wildflowers. The sky

was bright and cold today, winds
thoughtless as my blood still
pumping. This is not the first time.

I've decided by now that if ever there was
something fine inside me, it is broken now.

If ever I carried something—a vase,
say, or a delicate glass bird—it has shattered
long before this. I have enough:

a long dark funeral coat, strong fingers
and a knife for slicing open the bag

of well-enriched soot. There are prayers
but they stick in the throat. Useless, bent—
if there was hope, its need has passed.

We are as it is, ragged as wolves
in the common daylight. Aware

of the weight of each breath, measuring
whether the heart should follow.
If there is salvation, I do not want it.

If there was water, it has frozen.
If there was memory, something ancient

and ancestral as the curl of fins,
if we stirred in the deep, it is finished.
We are houses propped by grief.

If there is God, keep him away—
do not relieve me of anything.

# THE SUBSTITUTE

A fourteen-year-old girl opens
her fist, flat on the desk,
and lets a bully rub a Paper Mate eraser

over the thin rivulets of her palm,
back and forth until pink
cinders form a pile, leaving behind

an egg-sized scar over the wilted
violet of her lifeline. I want to
check back in a few years, ask how it feels

threading that backwater tattoo
through the sleeve of a prom dress,
fielding questions

from strangers on a plane
or a neighbor on the factory line.
Instead, I ask her why.

*To show him I'm tough,* she says.
Her eyes meet mine. Dry, unblinking,
and I am afraid to say more.

# ODE TO CONTROL-Z

I am teaching my class
   the proper keystroke

to reverse what they've done
on their PCs
     in case they make a mistake

or their formatting goes to hell
when I think
how useful this would be
in real life—

one finger-flick to take back
when I blamed our fights on your mother

or accused you of gaining weight
     in the wrong places;

two more for those petulant emails
I sent while drunk—the same

for my uncast vote, wet shards
on the kitchen floor, all the cats and rabbits

I've stamped onto star-lit highways
in my dumb, terrible rush

to get from state to state,
   figurative to literal,
      numb to just before.

## NOT EVEN IN MY DREAMS

My friend says that in his dreams,
he hunts down vampires
and beds more women than James Bond.
I don't have the nerve
to tell him that in mine, I only break up
bar fights or get my keys stolen.
And if a beautiful woman is involved,
one whose dark eyes leave
astronomers speechless, always
she leaves me for a rapper
or a prince who smirks from the door
of an immaculate white limousine
while I clear their dirty dishes.
Even tonight, belly-down
in my crow's nest, rifle-scope trained
on the brow of some dictator
famous for bombing orphanages,
something in me stalls—notes instead
the symmetry of his tanks,
his children playing, the laughter
of sunlight on his medals.
Then, the woman who tip-toes out
of the compound and whispers something
naughty into the pink seashell

of his ear—something that makes him
blush, beautifully glad to be alive.

# PECCADILLO

Let me confess how, for years,
I mistook *peccadillo*, that Spanish noun
referring to a slight offense

or, in modern times, a quirky trait
for *packofdildos*, three slurred
words forming a kind of postmodern kenning.

Once, in a crowded diner,
my friend bragged how his wife loved him
in spite of his packofdildos,

which I imagined her withdrawing
with mild surprise from under
his mattress or out of a chest in the closet.

*How strangely sweet*, I thought,
weathering the awkward turn afforded
by his uncharacteristic openness

to appreciate his good fortune.
It is hard, after all, to find accepting mates—
a truth witnessed each day

by tabloids and divorce lawyers. Then on,
more vividly than I wanted to,
I imagined them meeting

at the close of a long day
by the lamplight of their bedroom,
the blinds closed, the backdoor locked,

his infamous packofdildos in hand.
Sometimes, the question arises: *glass or plastic?*
What colors of the rainbow

they favor, nightly threading
bliss through love's small, unblinking eye,
cross-stitching their quirks

till death's banality does them part.

## INTERSECTION

There is something beautiful
about a young woman you don't know

sneezing as she speeds
through a burgundy traffic light—

especially if it's seven in the morning
and you're still hung over

from another night spent trying
to make this life explicable.

See how her blond tresses fold
like Easter ribbons; how she winces,

a cherub mid-seizure, red mittens
steering her on to wherever.

How gracefully she breaks the law
with her eyes closed, wisely

knowing better than to look back
at us fools she leaves behind.

## RACISM BETWEEN LOVERS

In the morning, you throw
your wet, olive arms

around my pale shoulders
as we're showering and

say: *I'm only pretending*
*to love you for the green card,*

our old joke, me born
in Iowa City, you in Chicago

to Filipino sweethearts
who kneaded Tagalog rosaries

as you played Tom Waits,
chose french fries over

buried fermented egg,
introduced me in Baguio City

as the *cauc* to your *asian,*
your grandmother wincing,

so I say: *I'm only with you*
*because you have slanty eyes,*

those almond windows
into your paper crane soul flashing

as you lean further
and we share a kiss that,

despite my bad jokes,
tastes nothing like soy sauce.

## DEAR JULIAN

I have no idea how to tell you this,
but I was the one who urged your mother
that you not be born. It was March,

wintermelt had me feeling more
cautious than I'm used to, and she had
a weak heart, as you may recall

from sleeping beneath its drum-beat.
I sided with doctors. We all meant well.
Besides, there was talk you might

emerge a bit on the mangled side,
and I know from my own maker's gaze
how awful a burden love can be.

I am not trying to apologize here.
That you screamed, turned pink, slept—
mere chance. *Chance*, that term

for what vaults us naked into glare,
where the sun drips like a glacier
and continents kick each other for sport.

Or *adaptation*—another graceless word,
and I know it's small comfort to hear
we might have gone on fine without you,

but it's October now. Gypsy leaves
patter off the window while you nurse
in the cruelty of a pumpkin costume.

She says you need to be changed,
last night's milk having run its course.
But for a moment, I am not sure

if it's you, or a hint of the soil-fed trees
ghosting sweetly through the glass,
perfumed by yesterday's loss.

## ON THE OCCASION OF TWO POETS COMMITTING SUICIDE IN THE SAME MONTH

Staying alive is what hurts.
Not the moment when the heart
stutters, but afterwards,
when the body tries to shove itself
along like nothing happened.
Not the punch, the crash,
the bullet, but our wild response—
blood rerouted, adrenaline
flooding abruptly lacerated tissues.
All not to soothe, of course,
but to make you mad. To keep you
going. This is what hurts.
Walking with shrapnel
from a Ford Pinto
or a smart bomb in your leg.
Walking without a leg.
Same can be said about loss—
not the moment when
someone you cherish goes extinct,
but that moment
when you tighten your gut
and go to the grocery store without them.
When you drive by the bar
where you told your deepest secrets
to someone you trusted
not to leave. Least of all like that.

## LATE SEPTEMBER

Dusk crayons the bay windows
near the pressboard desk where I work,
and for a moment, I stop
                        and listen
to the smooth, parabolic whine
of a motorcycle
                        braiding its own exhaust
down a few seconds of highway
running outside my house.
                        This is all I will ever know
about the cycle's anonymous driver:
that one Sunday
in late September, he or she
            maybe under a carbon fiber helmet
broke the speed limit
while I too wrote left to right.
Both of us
                        crossing the blank page
we fill, just because we can.

# Acknowledgments

*Arts & Letters*: "Limbic Self-Loathing, Post Emperor's Chicken," "Late September"

*Asimov's Science Fiction Magazine*: "Into the Deep," "The First Dancers"

*caesura*: "The Last Good American Decides Not to Run for President"

*Fugue*: "The First Kill"

*Hiss Quarterly*: "Jesus Returns to the World with Amnesia and Tries to Live a Normal Life"

*MARGIE*: "The Crayon Not Taken," "Blue Collar Eulogy," "Collateral Damage," "Elegy for a Horse's Ass"

*Mid-American Review*: "Ode to Dogs"

*Mythic Delirium*: "Scientists Discover Singing Iceberg in Antarctica"

*National Poetry Review*: "The Trouble with Hammers," "Diagnosing God"

*Ploughshares*: "The Clay-Shaper's Husband," "Against Etymology"

*Re)verb*: "Ode to a Trojan"

*River Styx*: "Samsara," "Peccadillo"

*Sometimes City*: "Grief Song"

*Terminus Magazine*: "Real Courage"

*Tupelo Press Poetry Project*: "Snowman"

"The Trouble With Hammers" won the 2006 Annie Finch Prize for Poetry from *National Poetry Review* and also appeared on *Verse Daily*.

"Ode to Dogs" won the 2006 James Wright Poetry Award from *Mid-American Review*.

"Diagnosing God" won the 2007 Laureate Prize for Poetry from *National Poetry Review*.

"The First Kill" won second place in the Fifth Annual *Fugue* Poetry Contest.

Some of these poems also appeared, occasionally in different form, in *Cardboard Urn*, *The Right Madness of Beggars*, *Real Courage*, and *The Clay-Shaper's Husband*, limited edition chapbooks from Southeast Missouri State University Press, Uccelli Press, Jeanne Duval Editions, and Codhill Press, respectively.

Michael Meyerhofer's first book, *Leaving Iowa*, won the Liam Rector First Book Award. He has also published three chapbooks and recently received the James Wright Poetry Award, the Annie Finch Prize, and the Laureate Prize. He teaches at Ball State University in Indiana.

CPSIA information can be obtained
at www.ICGtesting.com
Printed in the USA
FFOW01n2226121014
7938FF